Ok, So What Will You Learn?

- What Is Affiliate Marketing
- Affiliate Marketing In 3 Steps
- Affiliate Marketing Businesses Vs Sole Ownership
- So Many Affiliate Programs! Which One Do I Choose?
- Affiliate Marketing: Staying Away From Scams
- Which Affiliate Networks To Look Out For When Promoting
- 3 Easy-to-do Steps In Getting Started In Affiliate Marketing
- Finding Hot Selling Products To Sell
- Pitfalls To Avoid When Starting Your Affiliate Marketing Business
- Other Notable Common Affiliate Marketing Mistakes
- Here's How To Avoid The 3 Most Common Affiliate Mistakes
- Is It Worth Buying Affiliate Software?
- Website Or No Website...that's The Question
- What Affiliate Marketing Mentors To Follow, And Why?
- Techniques In Affiliate Marketing Done By The Best
- Keyword Research That Works
- Search Engine Optimization For Affiliate Marketers
- Top Seven Ways Writing Articles Can Explode Your Business
- Using An Ad Tracker Is Key To The Affiliate Marketer
- Using Product Recommendations To Increase Your Bottom Line
- Here's Why Using Camtasia Can Increase Your Affiliate Checks
- How To Incorporate Adsense Into Your Affiliate Marketing
- Affiliate Marketing And Revenue Sharing
- Back End Affiliate Marketing
- Creating Multiple Streams Of Affiliate Marketing Income
- Why So Many People Fail In Affiliate Marketing
- Protecting Your Affiliate Commissions
- How To Become A Clickbank Super Affiliate
- Top 3 Ways To Boost Your Affiliate Commissions Overnight
- Overachieving Your Way To Super Affiliate Stardom
- Money Making Tips
- Final Words & Recommendations

© 2010 JustMelPublishing.com

What Is Affiliate Marketing?

Affiliate Marketing is a way of promoting online business through affiliate programs and advertising that pay the affiliate (or publisher) a type of commission based on the amount of business their website brings the merchant company.

It's a form of revenue sharing or commission based advertising. The term "affiliate marketing," however, is often associated with network marketing or multi-level marketing and therefore many companies prefer to use the term "performance marketing". Affiliate marketing is the most cost effective sort of marketing there is, and is actually incredibly efficient. For this reason, many companies (especially those that started in the early days of e-commerce) owe a tremendous amount to affiliate marketing (amazon.com is a good example) and it has now become normal for companies to include affiliate marketing in many of their plans.

There are three types of compensation methods that are associated with affiliated marketing. The first type is Cost per Click (CPC) or Cost per Mil (CPM.) Basically, the affiliate earns by how many clicks the advertising on hisher site generates, or by just having the advert published on the website. But because of click fraud and many other questionable tactics, CPC is no longer the general form used for affiliate marketing. Generally, companies now either use CPA (Cost per Action) or CPS (Cost per Sale.) The first is based on how much the advert generates interest by the clicker to actually buy or register at the advertised site, the second is based strictly on sales. In other words, an affiliate is paid if the clicker actually purchases something on the advertised site.

Interested in learning more? Head on over to this kick butt <u>article directory</u>.

You can find thousands of <u>free articles</u> or submit one of your own!

Affiliate marketing is a process where the merchant will pay a portion of their sales revenue to an affiliate if the sale is result of the affiliate's promotion to the products and services offered by the merchant.

Now days, it's one of the fastest growing industries because it's cost efficient and quantifiable for both the affiliate and the merchant. Other players can profit as well, such as the affiliate network or the affiliate solutions provider.

The best benefit for the merchant is the fact that he will gain opportunities to advertise his products to a much larger market, therefore increasing his chances to earn. The more affiliates the merchant obtains, the more sales he can expect.

With the merchant having affiliates market his products and services, he will save himself time, effort, and money in looking for markets as well as customers. The affiliate marketer will benefit from each customer that clinks on the link in his website and who actually purchases a product from the merchant.

If you have wanted to join the growing legion of affiliate marketers and have an unlimited potential for income, simply follow these 3 steps to start an effective affiliate marketing program.

1. Identify something that interests you or you feel very passionate about. Then, focus on a specific area you know a lot about, as this will help you bring out your best and give your visitors who are possible buyers a demonstration of your expert in this field. This way, you'll gain their trust and encourage them to

buy the products that you endorse.

2. Search for merchants and products or services that are related to your interest then create a web site with top level domain names and very reliable hosting. When you choose the products for your web site, you need to consider the commission structure and the conversion rate.

There are many different affiliate networks and affiliate solution providers where you can obtain the information on most profitable products and which merchants pay the best. Take your time - and be sure you choose the right one.

3. Now, you are ready to promote. You've chosen everything you need and even created your very own website. You'll need to be creative, flexible, and willing to embrace new ideas. By this stage, you'll be well on your way to making more money than you ever imagined - and enjoying every minute of it.

Affiliate Marketing Businesses Vs Sole Ownership

Today, many of us want to back in our jobs and go to work for ourselves. However, the difference between those who want it and those that actually do it is staggering. Those that do make the attempt have two options open to them: create their own sole proprietorship or create and affiliate marketing business. Both can be quite productive if they are successful.

Business requires a great deal of work despite the avenue you take. The more you're put in the more you are likely to get back. However, the sole proprietorship requires much more time and commitment and a much greater degree of risk. Creating your own business is extremely difficult. Unless you have a unique idea that is marketable you are going to have competition with other businesses. You have to create strategies to attract customers away from the already well known businesses in your area and over to yours. If you succeed the rewards can be immense but if you fail you could loose everything.

Affiliate marketing businesses provide several advantages in this area. First, you are marketing products that are already in existence. Fairly known brands are not so hard to sell especially if they have a good reputation. Good and trusted products will attract customers much faster than something new and unknown. Affiliate marketing takes care of all of this for you.

Being a sole proprietor is incredibly risky. If your business fails like the vast majorities do your source of income has ended. Depending on how much debt your business had and how your financed the venture, you could loose much more than income.

Affiliate marketing takes the risk away. You paid according to how well you perform. You do not need to worry how the business is performing overall. You get your commission based on what you sell. Affiliate marketing businesses are usually well established so you don't have to worry about them folding up at a moment's notice.

Advertising is a huge part of any business. If you're a sole proprietor, advertising depends on you. You have to have enough in your budget to hire someone or devise a campaign yourself. The first costs money and the latter requires a great deal of time.

With affiliate marketing, the advertising is taken care of for you. You're usually given all you need in the form of leaflets, catalogs and other product information. You also likely gave good advice on how best to sell the products. Affiliate marketing programs should try to help you as much as possible. They better you do the better they do.

Finally, many times you need support and advice when you run a business. If you're a sole proprietor, you'll have to hire out professionals for this. This runs into extra costs for your business. With affiliate marketing, there should be a representative on hand that you can contact for support and advice. This service is usually free to all members.

Business is tough no matter how you slice it. Either route you take will require hard work and dedication. However, if you want to work for yourself, why not join a program where most of the work is done for you. With affiliate marketing, the risk is taken away. This allows you time to concentrate on what needs to be done. Making profits and creating your business.

So Many Affiliate Programs! Which One Do I Choose?

Ask questions first before you join an affiliate program. Do a little research about the choices of program that you intend to join into. Get some answers because they will be the deciding point of what you will be achieving later on.

Will it cost you anything to join? Most affiliate programs being offered today are absolutely free of charge. So why settle for those that charge you some dollars before joining.

When do they issue the commission checks? Every program is different. Some issue their checks once a month, every quarter, etc. Select the one that is suited to your payment time choice. Many affiliate programs are setting a minimum earned commission amount that an affiliate must meet or exceed in order for their checks to be issued.

What is the hit per sale ratio? This is the average number of hits to a banner or text link it takes to generate a sale based on all affiliate statistics. This factor is extremely important because this will tell you how much traffic you must generate before you can earn a commission from the sale.

How are referrals from an affiliate's site tracked and for how long do they remain in the system? You need to be confident on the program enough to track those people you refer from your site. This is the only way that you can credit for a sale. The period of time that those people stay in the system is also important. This is because some visitors do not buy initially but may want to return later to make the purchase. Know if you will still get credit for the sale if it is done some months from a certain day.

What are the kinds of affiliate stats available? Your choice of affiliate program should be capable of offering detailed stats. They should be available online anytime you decide to check them out. Constantly checking your individual stats is important to know how many impressions, hits and sales are already generated from your site. Impressions are the number of times the banner or text link was viewed by a visitor of your site. A hit is the one clicking on the banner or text links.

Does the affiliate program also pay for the hits and impressions besides the commissions on sales? It is important that impressions and hits are also paid, as this will add to the earnings you get from the sales commission. This is especially important if the program you are in offers low sales to be able to hit ratio.

Who is the online retailer? Find out whom you are doing business with to know if it is really a solid company. Know the products they are selling and the average amount they are achieving. The more you know about the retailer offering you the affiliate program, the easier it will be for you to know if that program is really for you and your site.

Is the affiliate a one tier or two tier program? A single tier program pays you only for the business you yourself have generated. A two tier program pays you for the business, plus it also pays you a commission on the on the sales generated by any affiliate you sponsor in your program. Some two-tier programs are even paying small fees on each new affiliate you sponsor. More like a recruitment fee.

Lastly, what is the amount of commission paid? 5% - 20% is the commission paid by most programs. .01% - .05% is the amount paid for each hit. If you find a program that also pays for impressions, the amount paid is not much at all. As you can see from the figures, you will now understand why the average sales amount and hit to sale ratio is important.

These are just some of the questions that needed answering first before you enter into an affiliate program. You should be familiar with the many important aspects that your chosen program should have before incorporating them into your website. Try to ask your affiliate program choices these questions. These can help you select the right program for you site from among the many available.

Many of us are upset and frustrated with our current jobs. The low pay and sense of being undervalued drive many of us to dream of our own businesses. However, the costs combines with the risk factors stops most of us in our tracks. Affiliate marketing is a way for people to work for themselves with no risk. There is no cost to you and you're paid on performance. However, today one has to be careful. There are plenty of scammers and con artists out there that are more than happy to take you money and hard work off of you. Unfortunately, affiliate marketing is not immune to these scammers. Daily, people are taken in by promises of big money with relatively little effort. In this article we will teach you some of the signs to look for and tell you how to spot a scam.

When you join an affiliate marketing scheme, you're either going to sell a product or a service. With products, you usually have a choice and range to sell. How you decide to do this is largely up to you. You could also sell a service. Web page designs as well as increasing sales and internet traffic are all examples of services offered by affiliate marketing programs.

How many times have you seen as ad on the internet promising huge earnings? Things like "Earn 1000$ a day" or "Join our program now and become a millionaire"... If you look closely at these ads they are not actually selling anything. Any company that is just selling the opportunity to make money is likely a scam. True, some affiliate marketing companies will have attention grabbing headlines like the ones mentioned above. However, if you go on to read the ad and information, there will likely be a detailed description of what they company sells. They will also have a disclaimer and terms and conditions listed.

These companies that offer, the opportunity to make money are likely pyramid schemes. The only people paying money in are the ones actually joining. There is no income being created, just money being passed from person to person. Not only are these scams and you'll loose what you invested, they are also illegal and you can face prosecution.

Another thing to watch out for is no free participation. If you have to pay to join then you may have stumbled upon a scam or what is known as a multilevel marketing program. Multi-level marketing programs are completely legal and some people make good livings out of them. However, if you're not successful you may end up purchasing a bunch of products that you cannot sell.

True affiliate programs are free. That is part of their attraction. There are no costs to you and they should also be risk free. Any Affiliate marketing programs that demands your money is not an affiliate program. You should ask yourself why they are misrepresenting themselves this way if they are legitimate.

Many of us dream of being our own bosses. We would love to be able to take control of our lives and careers. The attraction of answering only to you combined with setting your own working hours and committing what you choose bring loads of people into the affiliate marketing schemes. Affiliate marketing can be an excellent way for a highly motivated, creative person to make an excellent living. There are some wonderful programs out there just waiting to be joined. However, for every great program there is likely one that is fraudulent. Con artists operate in many areas and unfortunate affiliate marketing is not immune.

Before joining, check to see what the company is selling. If they are not selling goods or services then they are likely an illegal pyramid scheme. If they require your own money to get started then they are what are known as a multi level marketing program. Affiliate marketing can be a great opportunity but you need to do your homework.

There are many horror stories about affiliate programs and networks. People have heard them over and over again, that some are even wary of joining one. The stories they may have heard are those related to illegal programs or pyramid schemes. Basically, this kind of market does not have real, worthy product.

You do not want to be associated with these schemes. It is obvious you want to be with a program that offers high quality product that you will readily endorse. The growing number of those who have joined already and are succeeding immensely is proof enough that there are reliable and quality affiliate programs out there.

But, as we've addressed, there are many reasons to join a reputable affiliate program…

It allows you to work part-time. It gives you the opportunity to build a generous residual income. And it makes you an owner of a small business. Affiliate programs have already created lots of millionaires. They are the living testimony of how hard work; continuous prospecting, motivating and training others pay off.

If ever you are deciding to join one, you must take note that you are getting into something that is patterned to what you are capable of. This will be an assurance that you are capable of doing anything to come out successful.

How do you choose a good affiliate program to promote? Here

are some tips you may want to look over before choosing one:

1. A program that you like and have interest in. One of the best ways of knowing if that is the kind of program you wish to promote is if you are interested in purchasing the product yourself. If that is the case, chances are, there are many others who are also interested in the same program and products.

2. Look for a program that is of high quality. For instance, look for one that is associated with many experts in that particular industry. This way, you are assured that of the standard of the program you will be joining into.

3. Join in the ones that offer real and viable products. How do you know this? Do some initial research. If possible, track down some of the members and customers to give you testimonial on the credibility of the program.

4. The program that is catering to a growing target market. This will ensure you that there will be more and continuous demands for your referrals. Make inquiries. There are forums and discussions you can participate in to get good and reliable feedbacks.

5. A program with a compensation plan that pays out a residual income and a payout of 30% or more would be a great choice. There are some programs offering this kind of compensation. Look closely for one. Do not waste your time with programs that do not reward substantially for your efforts.

6. Be aware of the minimum quotas that you must fulfill or sales target that is too hard to achieve. Some affiliate programs imposes pre-requisites before you get your commissions. Just be sure that you are capable of attaining their requirements.

7. Select one that has plenty of tools and resources that can help you grow the business in the shortest possible time. Not all affiliate programs have these capacities. Make use you decide on one with lots of helpful tools you can use.

8. Check out if the program has a proven system that can allow you to check your networks and compensation. Also check if they have it available online for you to check anytime and anywhere.

9. The program that is offering strong incentives for members to renew their membership each time. The affiliate programs that provide continuous help and upgrades for its products have the tendency to retain its members. These things can assure the growth of your networks.

10. Beware of the things that members are not happy about in a program. Like with the ones mentioned above, you can do your checking at discussion forums. If you know someone in that same program, there is ho harm asking if there are many downsides involved.

Have a thorough and intensive knowledge about the affiliate program and network you will be promoting on.

Knowing the kind of program you are getting yourself into will make you anticipate and prevent any future problems you may encounter.

Affiliate marketing is said to be the agreement between an online business and an affiliate, in which the affiliate makes a payment for making sales, guides and clicks for the businessperson's website.

Affiliate marketing functions a condition, which is beneficial to both the business and the affiliate. The businessperson gets chances to promote his products without charge to a bigger market, which will improve the sales of his business.

The more reliable affiliates he find, the more sales he can anticipate to come. By looking for affiliates to promote his products and services, he is already reducing his time, attempts and money in searching for potential markets and clients.

As a customer clicks on the link in the affiliate site and buys the product, he or she suggests it to other customers who is on the course of searching for the similar item or purchases it again, this way the businessperson's influences his opportunity of profiting. Then again, the affiliate marketer gains from every client who clicks on the link in his site and who eventually buys the product or gets the service offered by the businessperson.

Normally, the affiliate acquires payments per sale made, which can be settled on a percentage or definite amount. The nice thing about this is that it will not charge a dollar to join in an affiliate program.

If you are thinking to be an affiliate marketer and earn money on the internet, you can follow the below listed three most essential steps to begin your efficient affiliate marketing campaign.

• The first thing you should do is to recognize a specific area you are fascinated with or passionate about so you will not be jaded and required to improve your affiliate site afterwards. Focus on a particular area you are familiar with, this will help you show your finest efforts and expertise. There are different places you can research on, so feel free to select a particular area you can learn more.

• The second thing is to search for a well compensating businessperson and high quality products. Create a list of well compensating and high quality affiliate programs for your selected area and make a site. In selecting a product, you should think of the assistance that they are willing to give you. This includes the promotional materials such as articles, links, banner advertisements, classified ads and so on.

• The third step is of course learning how to get the proper linking programs in your websites program. Also, develop your own strategies and methods to market the products and services.

There are many affiliate groups and affiliate result providers that can offer you information on the most moneymaking products and well compensating businesses available. Therefore, be clever enough to select the accurate affiliate program fit for you. Once you are sure about which products to market and the business to support and have made your own site with an area name and dependable hosting provider, you are prepared to do the promotion. This is the hardest part, since by mean of this you should be capable of enhancing traffic to the business website, sales and certainly, earnings.

In affiliate marketing, it is possible to make huge amount of money in the least period of time if you utilize the accurate techniques and ways.

Promoting a product would mean a different topic. You should be consistent in informing yourself by reading books, courses or important articles on the internet about the effective and proven promoting strategies.

Keep in mind, there is no fast way to success. Affiliate marketing may appear very appealing because of the number of encouraging statements of both the businesses and affiliate marketers who have gained from it. However, it still includes an excellent pact of effort and determination. You are also required to be resourceful and elastic.

There are affiliate marketers that do not realized this, so when they do not get sales, they give up, search for other affiliate programs and keep on doing the same mistakes. Then after a while, you will hear them saying affiliate marketing is only one of the rip offs existing online. You can surely taste the excellence of success if you use the proper techniques in affiliate marketing. You can earn more money as an affiliate marketer if you are determined to do the things it needed to work.

Above all, keep your intelligence and stay wise as you get started with affiliate marketing. Follow the three steps and it will surely lead you to the success you are longing for.

In order to locate products that sell online, we need to understand what people already want to buy. Finding a good choice of idea or product is always accompanied by interfacing the demand for the product in the current market and the level of competition or market share that the product will be having in the long run.

"What should I sell? What products are hot selling?" These are the questions most people are trying to find an answer in order for them to make the definite decision. And if we really want to know the answer to this question, our only choice is to do some research. There are all kinds of twists along the road that may lead you to think you have a high-demand idea. We must be able to understand and satisfy the need, wants and expectations of our customers on a certain product that they're trying to buy. This three are called the basic needs or minimum requirements in a purchase. Needs are the basic reasons or the minimum requirements consumers are looking for in a product or service. They are called the qualifying or "gatekeeper" dimensions in a purchase. Wants are the determining dimensions among many choices. Expectations, on the other hand, are values or intangibles associated with a product or service. Expectations are actually part of "wants" but they become extremely important when products or services are not differentiated.

For example, in reading a logic book, university students look for the following: Relevant logic concepts use of simple language, easy to understand and affordable prices. These similar ideas can be applied to Internet Sales as well. After all, the Internet is just another place to sell products. The basic concept of demand is the same there as it is anywhere else, and has been all the time.

Now, the second thing that must be considered in finding "hot" products to sell are the level of competition or the market shares do your product will have. Market share or level of competition means the ratio of your brand sales versus the total market sales. While companies would naturally define its target competitors, it is actually the consumers who ultimately decide the competitive frame, or the list related products or services that consumers consider when exercising their purchasing power. We must therefore choose the market segment where we can have a potential leadership or at least a strong challenger role. Because the overriding objective of getting into this business is not just to satisfy the needs and wants of our customers but to do so profitably better than his competition. Otherwise, our competition will end up satisfying the customers better than our own interest.

Third factor to be considered in finding hot selling products is finding out the general interest level about the product. General interest in a product helps us to gauge where our demand and competition numbers fall into the big picture. Simply saying, if there isn't much demand for the product, and there isn't much competition, it would seem that it might not be good a good put up for sale. But the research doesn't stop here; there is one last thing to be considered to exactly find the hot selling products that you've been looking for. We must also learn how others are advertising those products. If there are a good number of them doing so, it may mean that it's a good product to get into. Coming to the last phase of the process is analyzing and evaluating all the information that has been collected. We have to look at all of the data we have collected on demand, competition, and advertising, and make decision as how they all balance out.

And here are several factors or aspects that must be measured: (a) not enough demand means not enough people are going to buy (b) too much competition means not enough of a profit to go around (c) too much advertising drives up the price of pay per click ads, and competition as well (d) not enough general interest, combined with low demand, means there may not be a good market even if there is competition trying to make the sales.

Well, you have left that awful job and now are working for yourself. You have jumped on board your new venture which is affiliate marketing. You're incredibly excited and are working all the hours God sends to make this venture a success. You checking up and monitoring your site and you see that sales are going quite well. Many of the strategies and things that you put in place have helped your affiliate company sell quite a bit. The end of the month finally arrives and you're waiting for that first large payment. When you check your account you are slightly disappointed. You did make some money but according to your calculations you should have had more. You check your sales figures again and decide to contact the company. They inform you that some of the items sold were returned so those had to be deducted from your commission.

This is disappointing but it does happen. Companies do not pay out commission on returned goods. You need to be aware of this to avoid fall into further pitfalls. No one would expect to be paid a commission on a returned item however; some less than honest affiliate marketing companies can use this to scam some of your profits. You need to make sure you understand their return policy and how it will affect the amount that you are paid.

A return occurs of course when a customer brings an item back. Charge backs can also happen when they dispute an amount on a credit card. Be sure you keep a close watch on which items are being chargeback or returned. See if there are any patterns that are obvious. If you notice that the orders that are charged back are always very high ticket orders then they could be giving you false information. They are doing this to keep you commission down and keep some for themselves. Keep a close eye on returns especially if you think it is happening a little too often.

Charge backs are also indicative of another more serious problem. If you notice that many of these charge backs are happening during an initial trial period, or the money back guarantee time, then there could be further problems. This is a sign that the product or service that you are promoting isn't up to customer satisfaction. It could be misleading or just poor quality. However, it will affect your commission and your future as an affiliate marketer. If this seems like it is happening a little too often then again, there are problems somewhere in the company. Look to get out and make alternative arrangements.

You also need to be aware of which items are actually commissionable. Make sure you understand which products you will be earning money from to avoid disappointment later. Sometimes the company will offer a selection of products to put on your site, however only certain items may be commissionable. Before agreeing to anything like this checks your terms and conditions carefully.

Finally, you also need to make sure that items that are sold don't have any other conditions attached. Some will only pay a commission if the customer fills in the payment details immediately. If they select an item and continue to shop, you may not receive any commission on that item. You can also loose commission if the customer clicks on any other links before completing the order. If they order 30 of an item you promoting but click on something else then you have lost out on quite a large amount of commission.

Affiliate marketing is a great way to earn money. However, before jumping in head first you need to read your terms and conditions carefully. It may be worth having an attorney look them over for you. You need to be aware of the many pitfall people fall into when they go into affiliate marketing. Read and understand your terms to avoid disappointment later.

Other Notable Common Affiliate Marketing Mistakes

It isn't hard to set up a good website and start and affiliate marketing career. It isn't hard at all to find affiliate marketing opportunities on the internet. However, it is a very simple thing to make deadly mistakes that will insure your failure to thrive at affiliate marketing.

One of the most notable affiliate marketing mistakes is to think that all you have to do is find the ones that pay the most, sign up, drive traffic to that site through your affiliate link and you're all set right? Not exactly...

It's great to choose an affiliate program that pays a high percentage, but that's not most important thing to consider. It's much more important to find a quality affiliate program that meets certain criteria. Here are three mistakes you don't have to make:

1. You want to make sure the product is a proven seller. You don't want to waste your time and money driving traffic to a site that doesn't convert. Find one with a good conversion rate.

2. Make sure the site you become an affiliate for protects its affiliates, and has your best interest at heart. Look for one that provides banners, e-mails, and other tools you can use to promote the site. Also, make sure that there is only one payment option. As an affiliate marketer, you need to be sure that you will get credit for your referral. If there is more than one payment method, you can get shortchanged.

3. Do not choose an affiliate program that promotes an e-mail

course. Nothing is worse than becoming an affiliate to a site that's first goal is to capture e-mail addresses, and then tries to make the sale second. As an affiliate marketer, you need to capture e-mail addresses, then to convert that prospect into a sale. Stick with affiliate programs that aren't focused on capturing leads because it's simply not in your best interest. Build your own list, not someone else's.

Here's How To Avoid The 3 Most Common
Affiliate Mistakes

We've established that affiliate marketing is one of the most effective and powerful ways of earning some money online. This program gives everybody a chance to make a profit through the Internet. Since these affiliate marketing programs are easy to join, implement and pays a commission on a regular basis, more and more people are now willing in this business.

However, like all businesses, there are lots of pitfalls in the affiliate marketing business. Committing some of the most common mistakes will cost the marketers a large portion taken from the profit they are making everyday. That is why it is better to avoid them than be regretful in the end.

Mistake number 1: Choosing the wrong affiliate product.

Many people want to earn from affiliate marketing as fast as possible. In their rush to be part of one, they tend to choose a bandwagon product. This is the kind of products that the program thinks is "hot". They choose the product that is in demand without actually considering if the product appeals to them. This is not a very wise move obviously.

Instead of jumping on the bandwagon, try to choose a product in which you are truly interested in. For any endeavor to succeed, you should take some time to plan and figure out your actions.

Pick a product that appeals to you. Then do some research about that product to see if they are in demand. Promoting a product you are more passionate about is easier than promoting one for the sake of the earnings only.

Mistake number 2: Joining too many affiliate programs.

Since affiliate programs are very easy to join, you might be tempted to join multiples of affiliate programs to try and maximize the earnings you will be getting. Besides you may think that there is nothing wrong and nothing to lose by being part of many affiliate programs.

True, that is a great way to have multiple sources of income. However, joining multiple programs and attempting to promote them all at the same time will prevent you from concentrating on each one of them.

The result? The maximum potential of your affiliate program is not realized and the income generated will not exactly be as huge as you were thinking initially it would. The best way to get excellent result is by joining just one program that pays a 40% commission at least. Then give it your best effort by promoting your products enthusiastically. As soon as you see that it is already making a reasonable profit, then maybe you can now join another affiliate program.

The technique is to do it slowly but surely. There is really no need to rush into things, especially with affiliate marketing. With the way things are going, the future is looking real bright and it seems affiliate marketing will be staying for a long time too.

Mistake number 3: Not buying the product or using the service.

As an affiliate, you main purpose is to effectively and convincingly promote a product or service and to find customers. For you to achieve this purpose, you must be able to relay to the customers that certain product and service. It is therefore difficult for you to do this when you yourself have not tried these things out. Thus, you will fail to promote and recommend them convincingly. You will also fail to create a desire in your customers to avail any of what you are offering.

Try the product or service personally first before you sign up as an affiliate to see if it is really delivering what it promises. If you have done so, then you are one of the credible and living testaments aware of its advantages and disadvantages. Your customers will then feel the sincerity and truthfulness in you and this will trigger them to try them out for themselves.

Many affiliate marketers makes these mistakes and are paying dearly for their actions. To not fall into the same situation they have been in, try to do everything to avoid making the same mistakes.

Time is the key. Take the time to analyze your marketing strategy and check if you are in the right track. If done properly, you will be able to maximize your affiliate marketing program and earn higher profits.

Is It Worth Buying Affiliate Software?

Many of us dream of giving up our jobs and working for ourselves. Being your own boss can provide the responsibility level you want as well as the incentive to perform well. Running your own business usually mean lots of hard work but the rewards can be quite tremendous.

When it comes to starting a business, many people get scared. They worry about loosing that security that their job has provided. They also worry about the risk involved in starting your own business. The risk is worth considering being that anywhere from 70-90 % of all small businesses fail in the first year.

Affiliate marketing is a great way to work for yourself with minimal risk. When you work as an affiliate you usually sell a range of goods or services for profit. You will still have to work very hard to promote your business; however the financial risk to you is extremely low.

Many who have started their affiliate marketing businesses wonder about affiliate Software. They wonder if it is worth purchasing and what it can do for their particular business. The answer to theses questions lies entirely in the individual affiliate and the type of business that they have. However, there are some general things to try and consider before you shell out hundreds of dollars on affiliate software.

Before buying any software program, you need to apply some perspective. Software will not take a floundering company and get it into fortune 500. It is simply a tool to help you in various aspects of running a business. You will still have to do all of the hard work.

The software will only help.

Once you have some perspective, then you need to list your companies needs. How are you at keeping accounts? Could you do better with software? Many people do purchase software to manage accounts for them. (Especially when their businesses start to take off). Chances are you can do just as good of a job on your own but software will make it go much faster. You must keep in mind however, that software does take time to learn. However, once you have mastered it accounting software can help you keep track of your incoming money and outgoing at a much faster rate than if you were to do it yourself.

If you have a home based affiliate marketing business that is entirely internet based, you may want to consider website building software. Again, you may be able to do just as good of a job on your own. However, if you can't, this software can help. It will offer suggestions on how to make your pages more attractive and how to attract more internet traffic to your site. This can all translate into more sales or Ad revenue for you.

You should never purchase any software without previewing it first. This way you can tell if this particular style of software is what you need. Most places will give you a free trail, if not find someone who will. You could also find free software that you can download from the internet. It takes little time to put this onto your computer. It is certainly worth at least trying the free software. It doesn't cost anything and could save you money if it does what you need it to do. If it doesn't then you can always have it removed and purchase what you need.

If you have a knack for sales or marketing then perhaps you should consider the world of home based affiliate marketing programs. You can put your creativity, skills and expertise to work for you rather than someone who doesn't appreciate them. When your business starts to pick up, you may want to consider the purchase of some affiliate software. It can help you manage your accounts and increase your website traffic. You could find it for free online or get a free trail from a software company. What ever you decide, remember keep some perspective of what it can do. Software is only a tool it won't work miracles.

Do you want to make money through the Internet but you don't have enough experience or capital to start your own online business? You don't have to worry, for a lot of online marketing options exist for you to start with. One of these options, and shall I say the best, is affiliate marketing.

Affiliate marketing provides first time online marketers like you the chance to market something online even without having your own product to sell. All you have to do is to sign up with an affiliate marketing program, which is usually owned by an online merchant or retailer, and start picking the products you want to promote. As an affiliate, you are paid by the merchant for your services on a commission basis, that is whenever you have directed a visitor to the merchant's site and the visitor actually buys something.

Becoming an affiliate in an affiliate marketing program is often quick and easy, and for most affiliate programs, signing up is also free. But despite these and all the benefits being promised by affiliate programs, many people are still hesitant to get into affiliate marketing. One of the reasons why a lot of people remain hesitant is the lack of a website to start marketing his affiliate products with. This now leads us to the question of whether a website is required or necessary in affiliate marketing or not.

Many people say that one can do affiliate marketing even without a website to start with. Actually, one can really start promoting and marketing his affiliate products even without a website; and there exist a lot of ways on how this can be done. In fact, many affiliate marketing strategies that leads to success can exist without actually needing a website. Among these strategies are email marketing, offline promotions, writing e-books, writing ezines and engaging in online discussions like forums, chats, message boards and others.

*Email Marketing

Email marketing, or maintaining email lists, is actually the most popular affiliate marketing strategy that doesn't require the affiliate to maintain a website. In this affiliate marketing strategy, what you basically do is maintain a list of the email ads of your prospective customers and provide them with articles that are relevant with the affiliate products and programs you are promoting. Articles that you provide your contacts with need not always be promotional, for many individuals find such types of email annoying. Rather, it would be better if you provide them with something informative and just add small text ads that link to your merchant's site.

*Offline Promotion

There are many ways on how you can promote your affiliate products offline. Among the common medium used for such promotions are classified ads, brochures and flyers. Classified ads would generally work better compared to the other two because classified ads in periodicals often get a wider audience.

*Writing Free e-books

If you have a knack in writing, writing an e-book can be the best way for you to promote your affiliate products in the absence of an actual website. Just like in emails and newsletters, your readers would better appreciate your e-book if it is not too promotional but rather informative. Be sure, however, to make the contents of your e-books relative to the actual affiliate products you are promoting. And just like in email marketing, you can just place text ads or banners somewhere near the end of your e-book that links to the merchant's site.

*Writing Free Ezines

Ezines are publications or articles that aim to inform individuals about a particular topic. If you don't have a website and yet want to be an affiliate, you can well use ezines to promote your affiliate products or to insert links to your merchant's site. If you have a website, your ezine article may actually work well as content for your site. But since you have no website, you can just submit your free ezine articles to various websites that hosts ezines, like goarticles.com, ezinearticles.com and others.

*Online discussions (Forums, Chats, Message Boards, etc.)

With or without a website, you just can't ignore online discussions because they are great venues for marketing your affiliate products. In chats, forums, message boards and discussion boards with topics related to your products, you can easily find people who may be interested with the products you are promoting.

With all these strategies, it may appear that one really doesn't need to have a website to start marketing his affiliate products and promoting his affiliate programs. Well, starting in an affiliate program without a website may be easy, but getting successful in affiliate marketing without a website is another thing. While one can actually gain enormous success in affiliate marketing even without a website, it is a rare instance that "newbies" like you can reach the same levels of success.

Having a website is not really a pre-requisite in entering into an affiliate program, unless otherwise the program owner would require you to have one. But while this is so, I would still recommend that you have for yourself a website, if not now, then maybe at a later time. Having a website creates a lot of advantages in affiliate marketing. For one, it provides you a place where you can creatively promote not only one of your affiliate products but all of your affiliate products. With a website, you can also advertise your affiliate products to a wider market.

Again, having a website is not a requirement in affiliate marketing. But with the advantages that a website can provide, I'd rather have one for myself and make affiliate marketing a lot easier for me.

Affiliate marketing has been in the Internet industry for quite some time now and it is among the most popular tools used by many online entrepreneurs today. It is a great option for those who want to put up an online business quickly and cheaply. However, there is still a large number of the population who knows a little or even nothing about it. And most of the people who have just discovered this business usually assume that they can easily make big bucks out of it. Well, they're definitely wrong.

To be successful in affiliate marketing business is not an easy task and it will never happen overnight. It's just like an ongoing assignment where you need to find out and try various advertising strategies and tactics. This may even require you to sign-up with numerous affiliate programs just to determine which merchants performs well.

Another misconception that affiliates have "bout this kind of business is that they expect to gain more if they place about 20 affiliated banners on just one niche. Well it will not really work the way you think it would because once your site is flooded with too many banners, it will look like a link farm and visitors won't be interested and won't even bother clicking on any of those banners. So if you really want to promote several affiliate programs in your website, make sure that they jive with the theme and topic of the rest of the content on your niche. Bear in mind that three or four affiliated links in your site are enough, depending on the size of the web page.

There are also some who think that if they add affiliate materials to their site, they can receive sales right away. Maybe they just don't know that affiliate marketing is all about advertising. If there's no traffic coming to your site, how can you expect to get any sales? Remember that the more you advertise your affiliate link or the site where the affiliate links are placed, the more click-thru's these links are likely to receive.

If you want to be involved or you've already joined an affiliate program, but you have the above misconceptions regarding affiliate marketing, then, you might need a mentor to help you figure out where to start and what to do in order to succeed.

In the dictionary, the word mentor is defined as a wise and trusted teacher or counselor. Usually, these persons are experts in the field they are into. They can give expert advice and guidance as well as supervision to another person. So when we say affiliate marketing mentors, they are experienced counselors that have made affiliate marketing their specialty. Affiliate marketing mentors can be those persons that have already been successful in affiliate marketing and are always willing to share their experienced-based knowledge from the viewpoint of both the affiliates and the web merchants. And that's the reason why we come up with this page. It is aimed to give you the stuffs that affiliate mentors should possess and follow and why do they need these things.

Of course, it is good for an affiliate marketing mentor to know and apply some theories and generalities regarding your business but there's nothing more helpful and effective than telling the client what works today and what are the things that could probably work in the future and if the trend changes. As a mentor, you should be one of the sources of knowledge for your client and the first one to teach them on how to generate more affiliate income. You too, need to be knowledgeable and equipped with the keys to success for affiliate marketers as well as for merchants. And you should guide your clients as they try to do the things that can help boost their profit because once they do well in that business, it can be counted as one of your great achievements. This also makes you a successful mentor.

There are some articles on affiliate marketing that says, in order to be triumphant in affiliate marketing business, you need to encompass and develop these traits: persistence, patience and thirst for knowledge. And as a mentor, it is your job to help your clients take in these traits within themselves. Once they've already developed the abovementioned character, it"ll be very easy for you to explain to them that attaining success in affiliate marketing requires sweat, blood and of course, hefty time commitment. These traits will also teach them not to give up.

Moreover, before you train your client to be proficient in search engine optimization, link exchanges, email marketing, newsletter marketing, reciprocal exchanges and advertising in forums, you should first become expert on these fields. They will surely find it hard to learn these things alone and without supervision from the one who knows best. So make sure that you are knowledgeable on these things before you accept any invitation to be a mentor. Yes, being a mentor is way harder than succeeding in affiliate marketing but this task is very rewarding especially if your client become victorious. The failure of your client is your failure too so you must do your very best to be able to bring your client on the road to success. Again, it is never an easy task and there's nothing you can do about it. After all, that's what affiliate marketing mentors are for.

Techniques In Affiliate Marketing Done By The Best

The percentage behind affiliate marketing is that:

20 percent of affiliates produce 80 percent of all income; while

80 percent of affiliates generate 20 percent of all income.   Ironic but true. You would almost certainly want to be one of those 20 percent that is earning the 80 percent of the total earnings. Who wouldn't?

Follow these basic steps and you will find yourself sharing the profits that the most fortunate ones are getting.

1. The best affiliate marketer cover their web site links. Cloaking affiliate links may not seem necessary, but it actually is. Apparently, visitors will not tend to click on your link when they see that it is leading to an affiliate program on your site once they point their mouse over them.

The usual tendency is for them to go directly to the affiliate domain. Thus ignoring your affiliate ID from the URL displayed. The best way to avoid this problem is by covering your URL. There are cloaking tools available over the Internet that you can take advantage of.

2. Successful affiliate marketers create and distribute their articles. Writing articles regarding your market niche is necessary to expand your reputation as a specialist in your field.

You can get the greatest benefits not just from writing these articles but also from getting those articles published and reprinted by other site owners and ezine publishers. Your articles will then give you both reputation and links from other web sites because of the resource box attached at the end of each article.

3. Affiliate marketers focus on a market niche. Loading your site with content that is focused on a certain product or service niche is one way of getting more web traffic in your target market. There are tools over the Internet that can help you point out market niches that is important for your website.

4. Top affiliate marketers use autoresponders. Autoresponders are important tools that make you capable of sending a timed series of email messages to those persons that signed up for them. Most of the time, these autoresponders are sent through by a third party provider. Look for the best provider that will cater to your autoresponder needs.

5. Smart affiliate marketers build web pages in order to pre-sell. Create either testimonial pages or review pages that talk about and pre-sell the product or service you are affiliated with. This is the best method of getting increased orders for your chosen affiliate programs.

Many programs truly offer an article or recommended text to sell their products for you and permits duplication of those articles with your links implanted.

6. An outstanding affiliate marketer collects email addresses. The best affiliates gather email addresses on their web site by presenting free reports thru autoresponders, giving out ebooks and newsletter signup forms.

This method is best used in building your own list of email addresses to contact. This also lets you contact potential customers that clicked away once they got into the affiliate program website.

7. Top affiliate marketers markets everywhere. You can advertise using PPC or ezine advertising depending on your market niche. Some categories of Pay-per-click can be expensive, but advertising somewhere is needed to get additional traffic to your site.

There are some good bargains in ezine advertising and some less popular PPC engines other than Yahoo's Overture and Google's Adwords you can check out.

8. Affiliate marketers optimize for the search engines. Search engine optimization is now getting more complex as new and more webmasters participate. But the basics put into your site can add to your visibility over time.

The most critical of the many SEO techniques is the use title tags that shows individual page content. Many webmasters write a master title tag and apply that site-wide. This is the worst thing you could do for search engine ranking.

9. Affiliate marketers have their own mailing lists. The best of affiliate marketers have their own newsletter or ezine and gather email addresses on their site to build their list of subscribers.

Having this list allows regular contact with potential customers interested in your site, your product and your market niche.

If you understand and make use of the above mentioned techniques, you can be one of the top people that are making it big in affiliate marketing. What are you waiting for?

On the internet, keywords are terms or words that relate to particular topics. Keyword research will involve various aspects, such as finding sales oriented keywords or driving maximum qualified users to increase their online sales.

Keyword research is the first step towards a successful search engine optimization campaign. You have to be very careful when selecting keywords, as it can be very tricky to select targeted keywords for a website.

The selection of keywords should always be based on various aspects such as product names, services, brands, or general terms. Often times, people forget about targeting geographical terms when they have global presence.

When doing keyword research, it's highly recommended to do a very thorough market research analysis to find the best keywords used by search engines to find products and services online - and find out what keywords are targeted by competitors who are doing well in marketing on the internet.

The first step in finding the best keywords is to make a list of the products, topics, and services that you offer. You can also make good use of your website logs to know which keywords have brought you the traffic in the past.

Be sure to select keywords that clearly define your business and products to drive traffic from the search engines. There are some websites which get high levels of traffic through general keywords although they might not end up being sales.

Today, users of search engines are aware of how they work, for searching products and services on the net. Users always look for the better products, locations, etc. Therefore, you should cover all terms for each - products, locations, etc.

There are numerous tools available which will help you identify keywords that are suitable for search engines. The challenge here is to determine which keyword is the best to generate traffic.

There are no secrets on how to rank high with the major search engines because effective search engine optimizations are now immense. What is search engine optimization? Before we discuss that thing, you have to understand first how search engines work and a bit of know-how.

Search engines are into providing their users with the most relevant and up-to-date information to match the search term that was used. They are sophisticated pieces of technology which allow users to quickly find relevant websites by searching for a word or a phrase. Search engine results are useless to users if the information doesn't relate to the search term, or if the results are old. People expect the most up-to-date and fresh information that is useful to them.

Updating your website everyday and adding some materials will help you get noticed by the search engines. So, if you are going to sell any type of product or service online, you have to optimize your website for the search engines, in order to boost traffic and sales. It is because over 90% of your business will likely come directly from search engine results. And for that reason, it is absolutely important to optimize your site for search engines for you to have the greatest deals in the entire world.

Search engine optimization (SEO) is the process by which webmasters or online business owners utilize strategic copy to augment their website's status. It is certain that the internet has grown so fast over the years and the competition for the best search engine position has created an enormous market.

Therefore, better understanding the fundamental elements of Search Engine Optimization is vital for an online business" success.

Making use of effective search engine optimization techniques will improve the page rank of your website. There are many tricks that can be used to increase page rank; the most effective method is to provide high quality content consistently. This seems like a simple concept but there are many websites that fails to provide content that visitors find interesting. Sites which provide content that are interesting, well-written and regularly updated create highly engaged visitors who are more likely to return to the website in the coming days. So, if you can set your website apart from those boring, lifeless sites then do it. You'll surely have a step closer to achieving high page rank through search engine optimization.

The next significant factor for an effective search engine optimization is to include keywords and phrases within your content. To make sure that you are properly targeting your market, you have to make sure that the keywords and phrases you have on your site are the keywords and phrase that your site is actually optimized for. The more keywords you use in your content, the more likely it is that online visitors will find your site when they do some research with those words. If you are unfailing with these techniques, then your overall search engine optimization will increase, boosting your page rank.

You should also have to develop a linking strategy as a part of your search engine optimization. Not only does this provide free advertising for your site, but it makes the impression that your site is imperative because of its affiliated links. For each link that you have pointing back to you, that is another chance for your potential customer to find you. The more inbound links that you have pointing to your site, the higher you will be ranked in the search engines.

Another is to develop a content stratagem. People who get to search from the internet are looking for information. The more information you provide for them and the more helpful it is, the more likely you will make the sale. Writing articles is the most effective way to build up content for your site. When writing articles to post on your site, make sure that you develop a clear means of arranging their content. You can do this by simply adding a new page to your site. This will allow room for extra articles to be added as you write them, and will allow you to build up an archive of articles which will maintain to draw online visitors. Make sure also that you have included your archived articles in a directory that is next to the root web of your site so that the search engines will catalog your online articles.

Always keep in mind that search engine optimization methods are important in developing your site's status. With that thing in mind, make sure that you write high-quality, keyword rich content and link your site to and from a deliberate family of other sites. These things will help improve your site's popularity and coerce increased business through your online business.

Top Seven Ways Writing Articles Can Explode Your Business

In today's highly competitive internet universe, the importance of attracting highly targeted traffic to your website cannot be overemphasized. Routing web traffic to your site can be your only means of survival, especially in the cutthroat world of ecommerce. Getting a high search engine ranking can be very difficult. Fortunately, there is plethora of website promotion strategies you can use to drive traffic to your website.

There is a wide variety of strategies you can adapt, from paid advertising to affiliate marketing. However, most of these techniques require payment. Nevertheless, there are ways to promote your website and increase your web traffic without spending anything. Writing articles is one of the best web site promotion strategies you can use, and they can be very effective. How, you may ask, can writing articles help improve your web traffic? Here are the top seven ways in which it can help explode your business.

1.Reach more people

When you write good articles, it would be a shame not to share them with other people. You can post your articles in your website or you can submit them to other sites such as e-zines and online publishers. By submitting your articles to these sites, you give exposure not only to your ideas but also to your website. Simply include a link back to your site or include your information in the resource box. With this, you get exposure and free advertising as well. Submit your articles to popular e-zines and take advantage of their popularity. Other sites who find your article relevant may also link back to you. Thus, you increase your link popularity, which is one of the most important strategies in the internet world. Remember that most people are looking for information online and by filling this need with your quality article; you may reap the benefit of more exposure and higher web traffic.

2.Free Advertising

Submitting your articles to other websites presents an opportunity to advertise your website without paying exorbitant fees. Although you should avoid marketing language in your articles and make it informative and useful to your readers, you can always include your site's link in the resource box. In addition, by making your article relevant and helpful to your readers, you are making a good impression for your website, which could ultimately lead to a visit and hopefully a purchase. Good quality content in an article is far better and more effective than a few lines of ad space. You have a very special opportunity to presell your product or service to your prospective customer.

3.Gain High Search Engine Ranking

Create a new web page for your article in your website. Optimize your article to make it search-engine friendly. Use top-ranked keywords and Meta tags that can give your website a high search engine ranking. As soon as you upload your new webpage to your server, search engines will spider through it and you can gain an increase in search engine ranking. Remember that search engine optimized content is a very effective strategy to gain a high ranking in search results.

4.Increases Link Popularity

Instead of looking for other sites who would want to establish reciprocal links with your site, you can simply submit an article to other sites. Just do not forget to include a link to your site in your resource box. When these websites pick up and publishes your article, you automatically get a link partner. Try to get as many link partners as you can. Link popularity is one of the factors used by search engines in determining search engine rankings. Make your article especially useful and appealing, so that more websites will be encouraged to publish it.

5.Optimizes your site for improved search engine ranking

By making your site keyword rich, you can greatly improve the search engine ranking of your site. Remember that keyword density is one of the most important factors that search engines use when determining the search engine ranking of site. However, you should always provide relevant, useful and pertinent information. Avoid the temptation of overusing keywords just to gain a high ranking as this may turn off most web surfers. Relevance and quality is still the most important things to consider when writing articles and it will be doubly useful to your site if you make these articles search-engine optimized.

6.Establishes a Good Impression and Reputation

By writing excellent, original and relevant articles, you not only give your site exposure, you are also creating a good impression on your prospects. Encourage more people to visit your site and do business with you by establishing an impressive reputation through your articles. Be seen as an expert in the field and your will ultimately gain more customers eager to do business with you.

7.Enhances your credibility through references and testimonies

Certainly, your articles are going to receive feedbacks and testimonies when you publish them in e-zines and free article sites. Record these positive feedbacks and comments and use them as promotional material in your website or in any of your advertising efforts. Your credibility will be greatly enhanced by these feedbacks, as it will create a good impression on your prospects as well as your existing customers. In this highly competitive world, excellent credibility and trust may be the only things you need to attract new customers or make loyal patrons out of your existing customers. Original, relevant, useful and pertinent articles are important tools you should utilize to improve and explode your business

Using An Ad Tracker Is Key To The Affiliate Marketer

There's a lot of money in affiliate marketing. This is true, however, only to those are seriously and zealously working on his affiliate program. Success in affiliate marketing varies in every individual affiliate and for the most part, it depends on his will and perseverance. No matter how good an affiliate program is, it will not prosper if the affiliate marketer does not pay the price of hard work. One must exert extra effort especially on the aspect of promotion. Nothing will happen if the links or banners would just lie idle in a web page, an affiliate must be able to convince the visitor to click it and proceed to the business site to buy the products. No click-thrus means no income for an affiliate marketer.

You can actually generate a full-time income by means of affiliate marketing and you can do it at home, and yes, even while you sleep. You must have a good web site to begin with. It must have good promotional and informative contents, pleasing design, inviting banner ads and all other important elements in an affiliate marketer's web site. It would be great if you have exhausted other means of advertising such as newsletters, email marketing, message boards and ad listings such as Google AdWords. You just have to go online once in a while to check your site and update it and to watch over the development of your marketing program. Does this sound so easy? It can be this easy if you have planned your affiliate program well and have taken all the steps towards success carefully and diligently. Now, there's a tool you can use to help you go through the program with ease and confidence, the Ad Tracker. For many experienced and successful affiliate marketers, the Ad Tracker is a key to a successful affiliate marketing program.   What precisely is an ad tracker? It is a marketing tracking software or program that allows you to trace and take note of every click-through made by visitors of your site and by other customers who got your referral link. There are ad tracking service providers as well, so you will just have to pay them to do the tracking for you. With the ad tracker, you can keep an eye on the progress of your marketing campaigns even offline. This tool or program is especially helpful if you are engaged in several affiliate and pay-per-click programs and have placed ads in emails, pop-ups and pop-unders, message boards, auto responders, Ezines, forums, several web sites, surveys and various ad service providers.

Of course, you don't want all your efforts to be put to waste so you want to make sure you are getting paid for your hard work. Likewise, you want to make sure every dollar or cent you disburse in your advertising campaigns is wisely spent. With the help of the ad tracker, you will know accurately how many and which of your links where clicked on, how many clicked on your links, how many of your emails were opened and how many of those who opened your email clicked through the business site and purchased a product, how many products were purchased, which of your banner ads or links brought the most leads and sales and many other pertinent facts and figures you need.

Sales records and all data stated are necessary in any business as this could determine if your affiliate program is still worth continuing. This would also help you determine which of your marketing strategies is most effective and which is most beneficial for each product or service you are promoting.

Every decision and plan you make must be well grounded on facts. That decision or plan of action may not be the best, but it is something not to regret about when you had valid reasons for coming up with such decision or plan. You cannot just decide to terminate your affiliate program, just because you don't earn big in an instant.

If you are serious with affiliate marketing, again and again, keep in mind that your success lies mainly on promotion and your hard work. If you don't seem lucky enough to convince many of your site users to buy the products, don't be disheartened and jump into a conclusion that your affiliate program is a failure. If it works for others, it could work for you, too. Know whether your advertising techniques are effective or not, which works best for your program and which doesn't. Get an ad tracker to help you know all these and you'd surely be on the right track towards success!

In affiliate marketing, there are many ways in which you can increase your earnings and maintain the account that you have worked so hard for already. Most of the techniques and tactics can be learned easily. No need to go anywhere and any further. They are available online, 24 hours a day and 7 days a week.

One of the more important ways of increasing affiliate marketing bottom line and sale is through the use of product recommendations. Many marketers know that this is one of the most effective ways in promoting a certain product. If the customers or visitors trust you enough, then they will definitely trust your recommendations. Be very careful in using this approach, though. If you start promoting everything by recommendation, your credibility will actually wear thin. This is seen especially when recommendations are seemingly exaggerated and without much merit.

Do not be afraid to mention things that you do not like about a given product or service. Rather than lose any points for you, this will make your recommendation more realistic and will tend to increase your credibility. Furthermore, if your visitors are really interested in what you are offering, they will be more than delighted to learn what is good about the product, what is not so good, and how the product will benefit them. When you are recommending a certain product, there are some things to remember on how to make it work effectively and for your advantage. Sound like the true and leading expert in your field.

Remember this simple equation: Price resistance diminishes in direct proportion to trust. If your visitors feel and believe that you are an expert in your niche, they are more inclined to making that purchase. On the other hand, if you are not exuding any confidence and self-assurance in endorsing your products, they will probably feel that same way and will go in search of another product or service which is more believable.

How do you establish this aura of expertise? By offering unique and new solutions they would not get anywhere else. Show proof that what you are promoting works as promised. Display prominent testimonials and endorsements from respected and known personalities, in related fields of course. Avoid hype at all costs. It is better to sound low key and confident, than to scream and seek attention.

Besides, you would not want to sound unprofessional and have that thinking stick to your potential customers and clients, now would you? Best to appear cool and self-assured at the same time... And remember; prospects are not stupid. They are actually turning to experts and may already know the things that you know. If you back up your claims with hard facts and data, they would gladly put down hundreds, or even thousands worth of money to your promotions. But if you don't, they are smart enough to try and look at your competitors and what they are offering.

While recommending a product, it is also important that you give out promotional freebies. People are already familiar with the concept of offering freebies to promoting your products. But very few people do this to promote affiliate products. Try to offer freebies that can promote or even have some information about your products or services.

Before you add recommendations to you product, it is given that you should try and test the product and support. Do not run the risk of promoting junk products and services. Just think how long it took you to build credibility and trust among your visitors. All that will take to destroy it is one big mistake on your part.

If possible, have recommendations of products that you have 100% confidence in. Test the product support before you begin to ensure that the people you are referring it to would not be left high and dry when a problem suddenly arouse.

Have a look at your affiliate market and look at the strategies you are using. You may not be focusing on the recommendations that your products need to have. You plan of action is sometimes not the only thing that is making your program works. Try product recommendation and be among those few who have proven its worth.

Here's Why Using Camtasia Can Increase Your Affiliate Checks

Since there are already lots of people getting into affiliate marketing, it is no wonder that the competition is getting stiff. The challenge is to try and outdo other affiliates and think of ways to be able to attain this.

There are also many tips and techniques being taught to these affiliate in order to best plan their strategy for their program to work effectively so that more earnings will be achieved.

What better way to wow your prospects and customers than to record and publish top notch, full motion and streaming screen-captured videos. Nothing like feeling your hard work getting paid by having your customers jumping up excitedly in great anticipation to buy your product right there and then.

This is Camtasia in action. It is a proven fact; giving your customers something they can actually see can explode your online sales instantly.

You do not need to have trainings and education to be able to know how this system can work for your affiliate program. Anyone can create stunning videos, from multimedia tutorials and step-by-step presentations available online. The process is like having your customers seated next to you and looking at your desktop, as you show them the things they need to see and hear. All this done step by step!

For those who do not know it yet, how does Camtasia works?

1. It can record your desktop activity in a single click. No need to have to save and compile all your files because it is recorded right there and then.

2. Can easily convert your videos into web pages. Once converted, you can have your customers visiting that certain page. Videos are easier to understand and take in unlike reading texts which oftentimes is a trying thing to do.

3. Upload your pages. Publish them through blogs, RSS feed and podcasts. You may want your Camtasia videos to get around and reach out to other people that may be potential customers in the future. Nothing like being visible in many sites and pages to advertise yourself and get your message through…

There are other things you can do with your affiliate program using Camtasia. You can...

Create stunning multimedia presentations that are proven to increase sales because all the senses are engaged. This also has the tendency to reduce skepticism among hard-to-please customers.

Reduce refunds and other customer issues by demonstrating visually how to use your product and how to do it properly. Complaints will also be minimized because all the facts and the presentation are there for the customers to just see and hear about.

Promote affiliate products and services using visual presentations. This is an effective way of redirecting your viewers straight to your affiliate website after they are finished with the video. Make the most of the presentation by putting your site location in the end and make them go there directly if they want more information.

Multiple your online auction bids exponentially when you give your readers a feel of what you have to offer. Based from reports, auctions that includes pictures increases bidding percentage by 400%!! Imagine how much higher it will be if it were videos.

Publish valuable info products that you can sell for a much higher price. It will be all worth the price because of the full colored graphics menu and templates that you will be using.

Minimize miscommunication with your customers. Instantly showing them what you want they wanted in the first place is making them understand clearly the essence of your affiliate program. The good thing about multimedia is, nothing much can go wrong. It is there already.

These are just some of the things you can do with Camtasia that can be very helpful in your chosen affiliate program.

Note that the main purpose of using Camtasia is to boost the income that is generated from your affiliate program. Although it can be used for entertainment and enjoyment purposes, which is not really a valid reason why you choose to get all through that trouble.

Try to focus on the goal that you have set upon yourself to and achieve that with the use of the things that may be quite a lot of help in increasing your earnings.

A lot of people are lured by affiliate marketing because it can be financially rewarding, even if you just stay at home. Affiliate marketing programs are best alternatives to those who are sick and tired of their arduous daily work just to climb up the venerated corporate ladder. You don't need products to sell, you just have to market them in your own web site and you don't have to worry about processing the customer's payments and the shipment of the products. If you are already into affiliate marketing, probably you were thinking about these benefits, too, before deciding to join an affiliate program.

Of course you want earn huge amount of commission. Who would not want it anyway? Keep in mind, however, that affiliate marketing cannot guarantee you instant success if you don't work on it. There are a lot of ways of maximizing your income. The Internet is a huge library of information; use it to learn of other opportunities and ways to increase your income. You can partner with several merchandisers and promote different products in your website; thereby, increasing your chance to earn a commission.

The easiest way for you to rev up your revenue potential is by incorporating Google Adsense into your marketing campaigns. What is Google Adsense? What are its advantages? How can it boost my revenues? These are some of the questions you might want to ask. Let's try to probe into Google Adsense, so you would know how it could help you in your affiliate marketing program.

Merchants place their ads in Google, which is one of the most popular search engines or tools for locating various resources in the World Wide Web. Now the Google Adsense program allows you to display these ads in your website and when your visitors click through them, you earn. The advertiser, which is the merchant pays Google for every click-through made by the customer and you as a partner of Google, gets a share from that payment.

What's great about the Google Adsense is that the ads are relevant to the content of your web page. Most likely, visitors of your web site are interested on the theme of your site and specifically, on the content of your web page. So, seeing ads related to their interest would definitely drive them to click through the link or the ad.

Using state-of-the-art technology, Google scans your web site and matches the content of your pages to their large database of advertisers; this way, Google is able to find ads that are targeted by the users of your site. In addition, Google changes the ads in your site as you change the content of your pages, so you can always expect the ads to be relevant to your site.

Having Google ads in your website is also a way of convincing your users to return to your site. Repeat customers multiply your income without having to exert extra effort to convince them again to click through your links. And your potential to earn doesn't depend on them alone. Since you already have their confidence, they can be your endorsers as well. They could refer your site to family and friends who probably share the same interests with them.

Advertisers in the Google Adsense program range from large international brands to small-time domestic and local businesses, so the targeted market for the ads can range as well. This adds variety to your site; thereby, attracting different kinds of users. As you attract more users, you increase your earning potential as well. If you are targeting a specific nationality for your site users, don't worry because Adsense can be used in different languages.

In order to boost your revenues through Google Adsense, you must pay attention to making web pages of high value topics. Make contents related to high-paying ads, so you can earn more. Some ads pay only a few cents while some ads pay you dollars just for a single click. You would need to do a little research on this so you can come up with a more relevant content. Join affiliate marketing forums and get tips from experienced affiliate marketers.

Becoming an Adsense affiliate marketer is easy and fast. You just have to apply online and once your application is approved, you can instantly set up Google ads in your site. All you need to do is copy and paste some codes in your web pages and in no time the ads will appear in your site.

Strike while the iron is hot! Take advantage of the favorable circumstances the Internet is offering you. Make the most of your affiliate marketing opportunities, use Google Adsense!

Affiliate marketing refers to an incentive scheme set-up by online merchants to generate sales and grow their business. Basically, those who sign up as an "affiliate" with the merchant receive revenue share, sales commission, or a fixed rate depending on the parameters that the merchant has set up. The most common schemes are the Cost-Per-Action (CPA) and Cost-per-sale (CPS) schemes – meaning that an affiliate is remunerated from a referral to the merchant only if the customer/internet user buys or subscribes to the merchant's website.

Some incentive schemes work on a Cost-Per-Click basis (CPC) which means that the affiliate earns when an advert is just clicked upon (or the user is redirected in some way from the affiliate's website or email to the merchant.) This is also closely linked in with the Cost-per-mil (CPM) method, where the affiliate is paid for just displaying the adverts on their site. Although these two methods only account for 1% of affiliate marketing, due to many fraudsters taking advantage of it and therefore becoming too risky for the merchant. The more common CPA/CPS schemes mentioned above bare no risk at all to the merchant.

Affiliate marketing owes its roots to the revenue sharing idea that has been around long before the internet. However, affiliate marketing itself was birthed in late 1994, when companies like CDNOW and Amazon.com saw this low-cost opportunity to grow their online business. The success of those companies proves in many ways the success of the affiliate marketing system.

Within affiliate marketing, everyone involved in the program will benefit. Each time the affiliate refers a visitor to the website of the merchant, he will earn income. On the other end, the merchant will produce sales without spending a lot of money for advertising and promotion.

With the goal being to earn more income, both the affiliate and the merchant should be considering the practice of back end selling in their business. Back selling is a great and well known support for affiliate marketing, as it can greatly comment the income that is produced from affiliate marketing.

Back end selling is the selling that's conducted after the initial sale. When a visitor becomes a paying customer for a product, another product can then be advertised and sold to the exact same customer, with the second product being called the back end product.

Now, the customer will already be acquainted with the merchant or affiliate, meaning that is already a level of trust between them. Therefore, selling the back end product may actually be easier than the initial sale.

For many years, back end selling has helped boost sales for both online businesses and land-bound companies. If the customer is happy with the initial product that was purchased, he'll logically assume that the online company is offering quality products and will come back again.

The normal technique with back end selling is to make the customer aware of other products, as these products can cater to other needs that the customer may have. When the customer becomes aware of the second or back end products, he will look into it and may make a purchase.

The technique of back end selling has been both known and proven to be very powerful in augmenting the income of many companies. Therefore, back end selling has made hundreds of online companies flourish and expand. If you use it correctly, it can work very well with affiliate marketing.

Affiliate marketing will attract many new customers and lead to the initial sale, while back end selling will build loyalty among the buyers. To put it in other terms, back end selling is a major ingredient in creating a winning formula in affiliate marketing.

Each and every affiliate should look into the financial promise of back end selling when it's coupled with affiliate marketing. The two of these can make the affiliate earn an amazing amount of income.

Have you ever heard or read the phrase 'multiple streams of
income" before? Do you know what this phrase means? For many
businessmen, creating multiple streams of income online or offline
is one way of securing themselves as well as their businesses in
the future. They also believe that it can also save them from the
so-called famine effect in the business industry. Once you are
engaged in affiliate marketing business, it is advisable if you have
multiple streams of affiliate marketing income so that if one of
those income streams vanished, it will not upset you the way
losing your sole stream would. If you depend on just one source
of income and this single stream has been downsized or has lain
off, you'll surely find yourself bankrupted and hopeless. Try to ask
the most successful online entrepreneurs and you'll discover that
they have established multiple streams of online income.

There is a businessman that said and attested that the very first
step you must take in creating multiple streams of income is to
assess or evaluate your resources. Start by assessing yourself
first. Jot down your answers to the following questions: What are
the talents, abilities, strength and gears that you possess? Are
you gifted with excellent and creative writing skills? Can you do
well at sales? Are you good in communicating with people? Are
you born with an artistic skill or unique ability that other people
don't have? Through this, you can determine the kind of business
where can possibly excel.

Next, look around and write down you assets and physical
resources such as computer, color printer, scanner, digital
camera, cell phone, CD or DVD burner. Write these all down

because it can be used as a resource. Consider also your friends and family. Find out what do they possess that you have access to. Remember that no man is an island. You can use the talents, abilities, knowledge and resources of everyone you know.

That's basically the initial step if you want to create multiple income streams. But if you're already a webmaster or a site owner, you definitely have an edge. Why don't you join affiliate marketing business to help you gain extra income out of your own website?

Being involved in affiliate marketing is one of the most desirable ways to make multiple sources of income. It is because affiliate marketing programs come in various shapes and forms. There are a large number of affiliate marketing programs that you can sign on with and start gaining bucks right away. In affiliate marketing, you can make money by promoting and reselling your affiliate products and by recruiting new affiliates. What's good about this is that you can find widest array of training materials that can enhance your marketing abilities. In affiliate marketing, you can be sure that there are genuine products to promote and sell and there is real income to make.

Either part time or full time, being an affiliate marketer is an excellent way to create multiple income streams by means of promoting products and services from web merchants. Here, you can get affiliate commission without investing big bucks in making your own product and without worrying about book keeping, customer support and ecommerce. All you have to do is to promote and resell the products and services in your site and pass on potential customer's the merchant's site.

In affiliate marketing, it is advisable to promote more merchants in your site so that your visitors will have variety of destinations to choose from. Using multiple merchants in the same site or niche means only one thing – you have multiple streams of affiliate income. There is absolutely nothing wrong with this business strategy because this is one of the best ways to protect your business and expanding your horizons. Through this, you can be assured that you won't experience crisis if ever one of your web merchants closed his/her program.

However, you should choose only those affiliate programs that interest you so that you can effectively advertise and promote them. Don't ever be tempted into signing up for numerous affiliate programs in the hope that one of them will bring income. Select wisely and don't be engaged in selling products you know nothing about. Go with the stuff that jives with your enthusiasm; your passion can capture your client by the nose and guide him/her to your affiliate link.

You should also work hard to make your multiple streams of income more stable. You can do this by embracing some strategies and tactics and by developing within yourself, some traits that can help you become successful in any kind of business such as patience, persistence and thirst for knowledge.

Lastly, just remember the adage that says "Don't put all your eggs in one basket." So that if one of them is lost, you can still have some to make omelets. And what do these eggs have to do with multiple streams of affiliate income? Well, it goes without saying that the more streams of income you possess, the bigger and better your money lake becomes.

*Why So Many People Fail In Affiliate
Marketing*

Affiliate marketing is one of the most effective means of generating a full-time income through the Internet. It's a fair deal between the merchandiser and his affiliates as both benefit from each sale materialized. Like in other kinds of business, a great deal of the profits in affiliate marketing depends on the affiliate's advertising, promoting and selling strategies. Every day, as affiliate marketing industry expands, competition heightens as well so an affiliate marketer must be creative enough to employ unique and effective ways to convince potential buyers to purchase or avail of the products and services offered.

Compared to traditional advertising practices, affiliate programs are more effective, risk-free and cost-efficient. But why do many people still fail in affiliate marketing? There are a lot of reasons and a lot of areas in the program to look into. The most critical aspect in the affiliate program is advertising. Many affiliate marketers fail in this aspect because they lack hard work, which is the most important thing in affiliate marketing and in all other kinds of business as well. Although it pays to be lucky, you cannot merely rely on it. Affiliate marketing isn't as simple as directing customers to the business site. If you want to earn big, of course, you have to invest time and great amount of hard work in promoting the products. As earlier mentioned, the competition is very high and customers nowadays are very wise, too. After all, who doesn't want to get the best purchase—that is, to pay less and get more in terms of quantity and quality.

Lack of preparation is also a reason why one fails in affiliate marketing, whether he is a merchandiser or an affiliate. Part of the preparation is researching. On the part of the merchant, he has to be highly selective in choosing the right affiliate websites for his affiliate program. In order to be sure he has the best choices, he must have exhausted his means in looking for highly interested affiliates whose sites are sure fit to his products and services. The affiliate site's visitors must match his targeted customers. On the other hand, the affiliate marketer must likewise research on the good-paying merchandisers before he signs up for an affiliate program. He must ensure that the merchants" products and services match his interests so he can give his full attention and dedication to the program. He can get valuable information by joining affiliate forums, comparing different affiliate programs and reading articles on affiliate marketing where he can get tips from experienced affiliate marketers on how to choose the best merchants and products with high conversion rate.

The website is a very important tool in the whole affiliate program. As an affiliate marketer, you should plan how your site is going to be, from domain name to the design, the lay-out, the content, and ads. Some users are particular about what they see at first glance and thus when they find your site ugly, they won't read through the content even if your site has many things to say and offer. On the other hand, there those who want information more than anything else.

Affiliate marketers with "rich-content" web sites are usually the ones who prosper in this business because the content improves traffic to the site. Websites with high quality contents—with relevant keywords and more importantly, right information about the product and not empty hyped-up advertisements—allow you to earn big in affiliate marketing even when you're asleep. If you won't be able to sustain the interest of your site visitor, you won't be able to lead him to the merchant's site. No click-through means no sale and thus, no income on your part.

Selecting a top level domain name is also crucial to the success of the affiliate program. Lots of affiliate sites don't appear in the search engine results because they are deemed by affiliate managers as personal sites. Major search engines and directories would think of your site as transient ones and thus, they won't list it in the directory. Before you decide on the domain name, know first what you are going to promote. Many fail because their sites are not appropriately named, so even when they feature the exact products the customer is looking for, the customer might think the site is not relevant and thus, won't enter the site.

Above all, an affiliate marketer must be willing to learn more. Certainly, there are still a lot of things to learn and so an affiliate marketer must continue to educate himself so he can improve his marketing strategies. Many fail because they don't grow in the business and they are merely concerned about earning big quickly. If you want long-term and highly satisfactory results, take time to learn the ins and outs of the business. Continue to improve your knowledge especially with the basics in affiliate marketing ranging from advertising to programming, web page development, and search engine optimization techniques. Likewise, study the needs and wants of your site users and how different merchandisers compete with each other.

Keep on trying; don't get disappointed if your first attempts did not pay off. Thousands are attracted by the possibility of generating skyrocketing incomes through affiliate marketing and so they sign up in any affiliate program without carefully understanding every aspect of the business. When they don't get instant results, they quit and sign up for another program and repeat the process of just copying links and referring them to others. When you sign up for an affiliate program, don't expect to get rich in an instant. Work on your advertising strategies and be patient. You'll never know how much you can get if you don't persevere.

There are numerous software products on the market that range from 15 - 50 dollars for special types of software that'll assist you in protecting your affiliate marketing commissions. The effectiveness and ease of use for the programs range greatly, so before you buy one, you should always learn as much as you possibly can.

- *Banner servers* - banner servers not only serve banners, as many of the more recent servers will also display text links as well. The link coding that's associated with served ads is normally long, so that the visitor won't be able to see on the status bar where the redirect is heading.

- *Click tracking software* - click counting software will not show the target URL as the links point inwards to the software, which is normally installed on your own website.

Once someone has clicked on the link, the click tracking application will then redirect the visitor to the URL that you have specified within the script. The click tracking software will also provide a great way to monitor the usefulness of your ads and not just relying on the reports that merchants will provide.

Protecting your commissions is extremely important, as you want to get paid for what you do. Even though fraud is possible with affiliate marketing, you can protect yourself. Fraudsters have certain techniques and tactics they use, which you can protect yourself from.

If you own your own business, the last thing you want to

experience is either credit card fraud or affiliate fraud. They do happen on a regular basis, simply because those who have it happen haven't taken the necessary steps they should have to protect themselves.

Making money through affiliate marketing is one of the most rewarding careers one could ever have. What's good about this business is that anyone can join and make their way to success. Affiliate marketing has been known to be cost-efficient, assessable method of conveying long-term results. In fact, you can start even with a shoe string budget. And with affiliate marketing, you can have the benefit of working from home and enjoying the freedom and flexibility of working for yourself.

But there are also some people who failed in this kind of business. It could be because they lack knowledge and tactics. If you are a web site owner and you want to join in an affiliate marketing business, you should know where to get good affiliate programs.

Clickbank is an ideal place to start. Here, you can find one of the largest affiliate marketing programs in the industry. You just need to visit their site, http://www.clickbank.com and secure a Clickbank ID. From the Clickbank's home page, proceed to "Earn Commissions" and look for the products and services that perfectly fit you and your site. These products are typically ranked according to their popularity.

Clickbank is one of the affiliate networks that serve as a 3rd party between the web merchants and the associated affiliates. It is responsible in providing the technology to deliver the merchant's offers and campaigns. The affiliate network also do the job of collecting commission fees from the merchant and giving it to the affiliates involved in the program.

Clickbank provides you a large and increasing network of publishers or affiliates to tap into. To be more specific, Clickbank has more than 100,000 affiliates who are experts in finding potential customers for your affiliate program. The reason why more and more affiliates are joining Clickbank is obvious – the process of gaining commissions in this network is absolutely fair and transparent.

For web merchants, joining Clickbank is so easy. You just need to sign up in their site for free and allow them to sell your products. Keep up a promotional web site that gives your potential customers detailed information about your offered product or services. At your website, you must also maintain a comprehensive technical support pages for your product. In return,

Clickbank will promote and sell your product, give customer service for your product, allow their affiliates to pass on traffic to your web site, enable you to encourage new affiliates to advertise your web site, furnish real-time sales reporting for you and the affiliates and send you and all affiliates a paycheck twice a month.

If you're a Clickbank affiliate wannabe, you surely won't find it hard to be a part of this network. First, you are required to place their link on your website and if you don't have a Clickbank account, you need to complete the Clickbank affiliate form and create your own account. Then, if you already have a Clickbank username, you are free to choose whatever marketing tools you want to use bring in more clicks and generate more sales. After selecting marketing tools, you can now get your affiliate link.

That's how simple it is to join Clickbank. But being a Clickbank super affiliate is no minor achievement. It means you need to possess the ability to sell lots of affiliate products. You also need to have expertise in search engine optimization, email marketing, newsletter marketing, reciprocal linkage, link exchanges and other methods of promoting your merchant's goods and services.

Among the secrets to become successful in affiliate marketing is to come up with good content based website and put your affiliate links in all your content. Your main purpose here is to give your visitors good quality content about the things they are interested in. Set aside the job of selling. It must be done by the sales letter page you are transferring them to.

Promote multiple affiliate programs in your website but don't promote everything the world has to offer. Just choose the affiliate programs that fit your site and focus on it. Then, it is advisable to automate the whole process, giving you more time for other ventures. Yes, you've read it right! Automation is another key to become a super affiliate.

Of course, you have to spend more time in reading, learning and taking up the changes in affiliate marketing business. Through this, you'll remain on top of the trends. If you are knowledgeable with online marketing, you'll understand how important it is to stay up-to-date. In this kind of business, what worked and what was accepted few months ago may not work at present. So always see to it that you know what's new in affiliate marketing every day.

It's really hard to be a Clickbank super affiliate, but you shouldn't say NO to the thought of giving up. Bear in mind that in affiliate marketing business, you need to develop persistence, patience and knowledge. These traits will teach you to carry on no matter how tough the job is. Also, check your statistics. This will help you find out what is working and what is not. Make necessary changes if needed but do it one at a time and be patient.

Don't forget that in affiliate marketing, everything won't take place overnight. And it will not happen without blood, sweat and hefty time commitment. Again, just encompass patience, persistence and knowledge; then do above mentioned tactics. Before you recognize it, you will start gaining profits. Believe me, the fruits of all your efforts here in affiliate marketing will be way too sweet.

Top 3 Ways To Boost Your Affiliate Commissions Overnight

The ideal world of affiliate marketing does not require having your own website, dealing with customers, refunds, product development and maintenance. This is one of the easiest ways of launching into an online business and earning more profits.

Assuming you are already into an affiliate program, what would be the next thing you would want to do? Double, or even triple, your commissions, right? How do you do that?

Here are some powerful tips on how to boost your affiliate program commissions overnight.

1. Know the best program and products to promote. Obviously, you would want to promote a program that will enable you to achieve the greatest profits in the shortest possible time.

There are several factors to consider in selecting such a program. Choose the ones that have a generous commission structure. Have products that fit in with your target audience. And that has a solid track record of paying their affiliate easily and on time. If you cannot seem to increase your investments, dump that program and keep looking for better ones.

There are thousands of affiliate programs online which gives you the reason to be picky. You may want to select the best to avoid losing your advertising dollars.

Write free reports or short ebooks to distribute from your site. There is a great possibility that you are competing with other affiliates that are promoting the same program. If you start writing short report related to the product you are promoting, you will be able to distinguish yourself from the other affiliates.

In the reports, provide some valuable information for free. If possible, add some recommendations about the products. With ebooks, you get credibility. Customers will see that in you and they will be enticed to try out what you are offering.

2. Collect and save the email addresses of those who download your free ebooks. It is a known fact that people do not make a purchase on the first solicitation. You may want to send out your message more than six times to make a sale.

This is the simple reason why you should collect the contact information of those who downloaded your reports and ebooks. You can make follow-ups on these contacts to remind them to make a purchase from you.

Get the contact information of a prospect before sending them to the vendor's website. Keep in mind that you are providing free advertisement for the product owners. You get paid only when you make a sale. If you send prospects directly to the vendors, chances are they would be lost to you forever.

But when you get their names, you can always send other marketing messages to them to be able to earn an ongoing commission instead of a one-time sale only.

Publish an online newsletter or Ezine. It is always best to recommend a product to someone you know than to sell to a stranger. This is the purpose behind publishing your own newsletter. This also allows you to develop a relationship based on trust with your subscribers.

This strategy is a delicate balance between providing useful information with a sales pitch. If you continue to write informative editorials you will be able to build a sense of reciprocity in your readers that may lead them to support you by buying your products.

3. Ask for higher than normal commission from merchants. If you are already successful with a particular promotion, you should try and approach the merchant and negotiate a percentage commission for your sales.

If the merchant is smart, he or she will likely grant your request rather than lose a valuable asset in you. Keep in mind that you are a zero-risk investment to your merchant; so do not be shy about requesting for addition in your commissions. Just try to be reasonable about it.

Write strong pay Per Click ads. PPC search engine is the most effective means of advertising online. As an affiliate, you can make a small income just by managing PPC campaigns such as Google AdWords and Overture. Then you should try and monitor them to see which ads are more effective and which ones to dispose of.

Try out these strategies and see the difference it can make to your commission checks in the shortest of time.

Internet business is a bit confusing especially if you're not really knowledgeable at it. You will also be left completely blank, asking yourself as to what type of online business is best for you. Why don't you try affiliate marketing business?

Affiliate marketing is defined as a revenue sharing relationship between advertisers or merchants and online publishers or affiliates. It is a low cost way for merchants to sell their products and services.

In this type of online business, you don't have to take any risk because you only have to pay the affiliate once the result is achieved. Once a customer is gained, a portion of the profit from that customer will be given to the affiliate as commission. Usually, an affiliate gets a commission for referring clicks, leads or sales to the merchant's website. The said affiliate income can be a fixed dollar amount or a fixed percentage.

From this simple commission-based referral system, some affiliates become experts on this field. In fact, some of them are gaining more than five figures every month. However, among the thousands of marketers, only 1 to 5% of them reached this level. And, if you're among the lucky ones who achieve this so-called elite level, you can now be aptly called a 'super" affiliate.

This means you are capable of achieving noteworthy percentage of sales or traffic on your merchant's website. Super affiliates are not only experts on search engine optimization; they are also great in newsletter marketing, email marketing, reciprocal linkages, keyword optimization, link exchanges, advertising in forums and other methods to advertise and promote their products and services.

But how does a person become a super affiliate? And how can they overachieve their way to super affiliate stardom? Making your way to super affiliate stardom is not that easy; and it surely won't happen overnight. Bear in mind that you need to embrace some tactics, carry out effective online business strategies and of course give hefty time commitment. You can't be a super affiliate without blood and sweat and without the following traits - patience, persistence and thirst for knowledge. Matched with efficient strategy, these three traits provide you the formula towards super affiliate stardom.

Affiliate marketing strategies are a bit difficult but they are achievable; you just have to work hard on it. First, look for a unique and exceptional niche and focus in it. The reason why most people in the affiliate marketing business didn't turn out to be very successful is that they try to offer almost everything under the sun instead of giving all their attention in a particular niche market. If you want to become a super affiliate, try not to scatter all your efforts; concentrate on your niche and make it grow by means of promoting, advertising and selling it well.

The next step you must do after you have established your affiliate storehouse is to promote it. Most affiliates resort to pay-per-click engines. But what's more advisable is to discover how to accomplish organic search results or better yet, hire a search engine marketing company. Through this, you can be saved from losing all your profits on pay-per-click engines.

Then, familiarize yourself with your product and know your audience. Remember that credibility builds trust. And you can only make information that puts up your credibility if you know the products and services your site is offering. If you're target audience don't trust you, how could you expect them to purchase from your affiliate storehouse? Moreover, if you take time to learn the products and services you are recommending, it will be way too easy for you to establish a website that converts well, which will enhance your affiliate income in return.

Try to promote and resell products from different merchants. There is absolutely nothing wrong with this strategy because it is just a way of protecting your business and broadening your horizons to be sure that you won't experience the so-called famine effect. Aside from that, promoting different merchants on the same site provides your site visitors a handful of destinations to choose from. This strategy will also make you aware on what your visitor want to see and it can also help you find out how well various merchants perform against each other.

As mentioned earlier in this page, a super affiliate wannabe should have this trait - thirst for knowledge. It is because this trait can help him or her stay updated and remain on top of the trends. If you are knowledgeable in internet marketing, then you know that what was adopted few months ago may not be applicable at present. So it is important to seek knowledge and make sure that you are updated on what's new about affiliate marketing daily. Keep in mind that super affiliates take time to read, learn and embrace the changes in online marketing business.

And what's most important? Never, ever give up. Being engaged in affiliate marketing business is hard, that's why you must be equipped with patience and persistence. Check your statistics and find out the things that are working and those that are not. Make changes if the situation calls for.

These are just few suggestions and ideas if you want to boost your affiliate income. Let me reiterate, you have to be patience, persistence and knowledgeable. Then, follow the above mentioned strategies and you'll surely find yourself on the road to super affiliate stardom.

Affiliate marketing is all about getting paid for selling products you don't own and not going to jail for it. ☺ Someone else goes through all of the trouble to develop software programs, service, or digital content products. They'll do all the work then you collect the money!

Affiliate marketing is a revenue sharing arrangement between the product developer, known as the affiliate merchant, and the affiliate marketer who is anyone that's willing to promote the sale of product by advertising the product using any type of legal means available.

The relationship will allow the affiliate merchant to grow their revenue by paying only for the advertising that results in a sale. The affiliate marketer will profit by making a percentage on a sale that he does not have to manage after the sale.

- *Getting paid* - all depends upon how the affiliate program is set up. Some merchants will run their own affiliate program. They'll have special types of software that assigns each affiliate marketer a special link that's used in promoting the product. The software will track sales of every marketer and the merchant will pay the commission on a periodic basis using either PayPal or another method of payment.

- *Selecting products or services* - Your income is directly tied to how well your selected product or service sells, and the size of the commission you earn, which makes it very important that you choose carefully when it comes to choosing the affiliate merchant you'll be partnering with.

Choose programs that you aren't embarrassed to promote and programs that you'll feel comfortable recommending to your family and friends if they were to ask you about it.

You'll do much better if you promote products that you fully understand and are already familiar with. This way, you'll be able to write better ads without having to strain yourself coming up with the right things to say.

You should only promote products and services for companies who have gone through the trouble to provide you with training programs and sales aids such as banners and other marketing materials that you can either use directly or model the one you own after.

Be on the lookout for programs with commission rates no less than 50%. You should give preference to programs that pay commission on multiple levels, which means you'll also have to earn commissions on sales made by people who buy the products through your link then go on and become affiliates themselves later on.

- <u>Affiliate Software Launcher</u> - Go from affiliate nobody to superstar in record time with this software meant just for affiliates.

- <u>JustMelPublishing.com</u> – Yup, shameless plug ☺ - Come join us and submit your articles, pdf's, and even videos to the coolest up and coming directory online!

- <u>SEnuke</u> – The most complete software available for marketing – so much so I myself use it daily! You can submit articles to directories & social networks, interlink your submissions, submit videos to the top directories (Google LOVES video☺), bookmark all submissions on the top social bookmarking sites, submit the RSS feeds to the top aggregators, and ping everything. On top of that you can research your next niche, find affiliate products, and so much more.

- <u>Micro Niche Finder</u> – The best keyword research tool on the market, bar none. Cheaper than a lot and well worth every penny!

- <u>Traffic Omega</u> – Worried about getting traffic to your site? This is the most innovative traffic getting plan to hit the net in years, & it's brand new so you know it implements the strategies that work NOW – not 3 years ago!

- And the MOST important recommended resource?

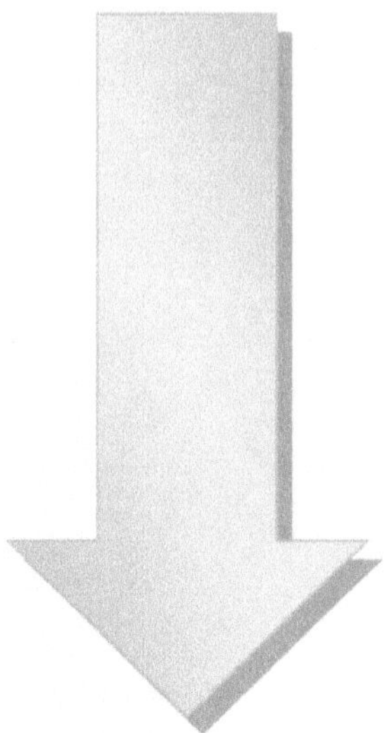

Nothing will ever happen until you get off your butt and take action, so get on it!